Josiah Sinclair

The Commercial Traveler

Josiah Sinclair

The Commercial Traveler

ISBN/EAN: 9783337292706

Printed in Europe, USA, Canada, Australia, Japan

Cover: Foto ©Suzi / pixelio.de

More available books at **www.hansebooks.com**

THE

Commercial Traveler;

A DRAMA IN THREE ACTS,

JOSIAH SINCLAIR.

THE

Commercial Traveler;

A DRAMA IN THREE ACTS,

BY

JOSIAH SINCLAIR.

CHARACTERS.

GEORGE W. McMILLAN, } Of the firm of McMillan, Baxter
AARON BAXTER, } & Armstead, New York.
ROBERT B. ARMSTEAD. }
HENRY WALTERS, Book-keeper.
CHARLES BROWN, Commercial Traveler.
CHARLES F. H. ULRICH, Packing Clerk.
DAVID CROSBY, }
JOHN McLAIN, }
GEORGE CUNNINGHAM. }
FRANK PEABODY, }
ROBERT O'NEIL. } Commercial Travelers.
RICHARD JOHNSON, }
LEVI ROSENBURG, }
ADAM BARNES, }
ALFRED HEADLY. }
MRS. CHARLES BROWN.
LOUISA NEINSCHWANDER, a Servant Girl.
Merchants, Lawyers, Citizens, Police, &c.

The Acts of this drama occur during the months of December, 1876 and January, 1877.

Entered according to Act of Congress, in the year 1877, by
J. SINCLAIR and W. MULHERN,
In the Office of the Librarian of Congress, at Washington.

THE COMMERCIAL TRAVELER.

ACT I.

SCENE I.—Office of McMillan, Baxter & Armstead.—Armstead and Walters in the Office.

Enter McMILLAN and BAXTER.

McMil. Good-morning gentlemen.

Bax. Any business this morning?

Arm. Nothing more than a few small orders. We notice the failure of Donald & Pratt.

Bax. Where do you notice that?

Arm. Under head of special telegrams.

McMil. Is it possible! they owe us twenty thousand dollars? What are the assets and what the liabilities?

Arm. Assets fifty-two thousand, liabilities one hundred and forty-eight thousand.

McMil. A bad failure, will hardly pay anything.

Bax. Have we any word from Brown?

Arm. No word from him, do not know where he is.

Bax. Well, if matters are to continue in this way much longer we might as well dispose of our stock and discontinue the business. An over-stock of goods and no one to offer them to the trade; our customers failing and no one to look to our interests—all, too, that our drummer may have a bridal trip. Other firms are pushing their business, but ours must remain at a stand-still until Brown, our drummer, has finished his bridal tour. Marriage is all well enough when the time and circumstances are favorable, but a drummer should not reckon his course in such a way as to interfere with his employment. Brown should not have presumed so much; he is our commercial traveler and business agent only, and should not be allowed to absent himself from his duties. Two weeks on a bridal tour and not heard from. The right course for us would be to employ another salesman and allow Mr. Brown to continue the trip for a life-time if he likes. We can get a better man for less money, and why not do it?

McMil. Mr. Baxter, you seem to be very much displeased with Mr. Brown, Mr. Brown has always been faithful to our interests, and through him as much as our own efforts we have been enabled to accumulate wealth from the profits of a good business. True he has been absent for several days, but then I do not think that he has forgotten us, and no doubt will return soon. At the present time it would be well to close out-standing accounts as they become due, but make no effort to sell goods on time. Other firms are trying to put their business in good shape, and it would be well for us to do likewise. The wise farmer garners his grain in view of a threatening storm, but the foolish husbandman allows his sheaves to remain in the field. We may not be able to avert the civil strife that is threatening, and should we be unable to effect a compromise of our political troubles upon a just and equitable basis then the country will be rocked by the tempest of civil war and our temple of political liberty may not be able to stand. However, as regards our business, a ship at sea can but continue the voyage, and we can only look well to our boat and drift with the tide of events. A strong demand for compromise is being made by those who are not professional politicians and who have the true interests and welfare of the country at heart. I am doing what little I can in the interests of peace, and I believe the demands of the people will be so great that they must be heard.

Bax. Well, as for me, I believe there is no danger of political strife—of civil war. The lawful returns have decided who is to be the next President, and all that will be necessary will be to concentrate a sufficient force to see that the proper man is inaugurated. The present state of the country doesn't trouble me in the least. We have goods to sell, and Brown ought to be on the road, or we should get some one to take his place.

Mc Mil. If we have business that demands early attention why not send out one of the boys, any one of them would like to go and no doubt would perform the duties satisfactorily.

Bax. I don't know which one we could send, unless it would be Herman, and he would be more of a surprise than a success.

Mc Mil. Well, suppose we let him try it. The fast line goes West at 3 o'clock, and he might be able to start by that time. Mr. Walters please ask Herman to come into the office. [*Exit* WALTERS.

Enter LETTER CARRIER.

Car. Letters! [*Hands letters to* BAXTER. *Exit* CARRIER.
Bax. [*Opens and reads letter.*
RICHMOND, IND., DEC. 23RD, 1876.
Messrs. McMillan, Baxter & Armstead,

Gentlemen:—You are hereby notified that J. G. Acker & Co. of this city have made an assignment of their property for the benefit of their creditors. Assets twenty thousand dollars, liabilities forty-nine thousand dollars.

Yours respectfully,

A. MORRIS, Assignee.

Mc Mil. That is bad news! It is to be hoped that our customers will not all fail. It would be well for Herman to visit customers of doubtful standing, if we have any of them, and try and put their accounts in good shape.

Enter HERMAN and WALTERS.

Her. Shentlemen, Mr. Walters zay you like to zee me.
Mc Mil. Yes. Herman is your name I believe.
Her. Dat vos my name, Charles Frederick Herman Ulrich.
Mc Mil. Quite a large name, and as we have concluded to send you on a business tour, we hope that you will be able to adapt your name to business, and if so, you will make a good report.
Bax. We don't want you to go on a bridal tour, Charles Herman Frederick Ulrich, we have one man on that kind of a trip now and that is sufficient. We will tell you where we

want you to go, what we want done, and then we want you to go and do it. You understand, do you?

Her. I go on te peesnis vat you tole me. [*Aside.*] May pe I vind Louisa, den I care vor not who tells any pody I vos gone on a bridal drip.

Bax. I guess there is no danger of a speedy marriage in your case, so you will answer our purpose. We want you to leave on the 3 o'clock train, and you had better make preparations at once. [*Looks at his watch.*] It is now 12 o'clock. We will make out a route for you and have papers and instructions ready by 2 o'clock.

Her. I vas ready in two hour and not zo much as vos dat long.

McMil. Herman, I will be absent when you return, and would say that when you get to Cincinnati, if Banks & Weddel's note has not been paid we will send it to you and have you see Mr. Carrick, our attorney, and try and have them settle it. Mr. Brown does not think much of them and I have been somewhat suspicious of them myself, owing to their peculiar way of doing business. If the note is not paid we will send it to you and we want you to make them settle it by paying the money. I will now bid you good-bye, wishing you a safe journey and hoping that you may have a satisfactory trip, in a business point of view, Always stop at the best hotels and take good care of yourself. [*Exit* HERMAN.] There is a special meeting of the Board of Trade for the purpose of asking Congress to agree upon some plan of compromise, and as it is expected that each member will be present, I will be absent during the remainder of the day. You can give Herman all necessary instructions; I feel confident that he will carry them out to the letter, and in the meantime we will have Mr. Brown's assistance. Give him a letter of introduction to Thomas Martin, and have him stop off en route and see him. Martin is an old friend of mine and a good customer, I promised him that we would stop at his place. Good-evening. [*Exit* McMILLAN.

Bax. Mr. Brown's assistance! If I had matters to arrange for the interests of the firm I would give Mr. Brown his discharge. The Board of Trade asking Congress to agree upon some plan of compromise! We want no compromise.

We will have Herman go as far West as St. Louis, and return by the way of Memphis, Louisville, Cincinnati and other points. McMillan and Brown talking about Banks & Weddel not being reliable! We have no more reliable customers than Banks & Weddel. Brown had the impudence to ask Banks for a statement of their affairs, but he learned they were worth a hundred thousand; we have no better men on our books, they are my customers.

[BAXTER and WALTERS *arrange papers. Curtain.*

SCENE II.—Herman's Chamber.—A poor but neat Room.—Herman arranging for the trip.

Her. [*Examining his clothes.*] Now I vas ready vor der drip, I wears mine goot clothes vat I brings vrom Shermanie, and vas a vashionable shentleman. [*Opens a large trunk valise.*] Dat vos one goot valise, [*Takes coffee pot from valise.*]. Dat vos one goot goffee bot. I make goffee on der drip. I go and show dem vot a Sherman man vos done. Der Sherman mans vas der schmarter den vos Americans. King Villiam vas a Sherman man; Bismarck vas a Sherman man; Von Moltke vas a Sherman man; Frederick te Great vas a Sherman man; Napoleon vas a —— Napoleon vas a Vrenchman; Napoleon vas one werry werry great man pecause Frederick te Great vas died; Schiller vas a Sherman man. I dakes mine guitar.

[*Sings while packing guitar and other musical instruments.*

"Wenn die schwalben heimwarts ziehn,
Wenn die Rosen nicht mehr bluh'n,
Wenn der Nachtigall Gesang,
Mit der Nachtigall verklang,
Fragt das Herz in bangem Schmerz.
Fragt das Herz in bangem Schmerz.
Ob ich dich auch wieder seh'
Scheiden, ach Scheiden, den, Scheiden thut weh."

Now I vas done and goes vor a gommercial drummer sellin goots. May pe I vind Louisa. Louisa gome vrom Bremen mit Baltimore; I gome vrom Bremen mit New York. [*Takes valise and coffee pot and examines his clothes.*] Dat vos one vine suit. Now I vas ready and pees gone.

Exit HERMAN. *Curtain.*

8   THE COMMERCIAL TRAVELER.

SCENE III.—Office of McMillan, Baxter & Armstead.—Baxter,
Armstead and Walters in the Office.

Enter HERMAN.

Bax. Well, Frederick Herman Ulrich Charles, I suppose
you are ready.

Her. Yes, I vas ready.

Bax. You was was you? What are you going to do with
that coffee pot—take a supply of lager with you?

Her. Mr. Baxter you make voolishness mit me, I make
some goffee on der road.

Bax. Suppose you allow somebody else to make the
coffee on the road, we don't want you to put in your time
cooking; it will be necessary for you to stop at hotels and
they will furnish you with coffee. Take these papers [*Hands
papers to* HERMAN.] You can read, and they will tell you
where we want you to go and what we want done. [*Takes
money from drawer and counts one hundred dollars.*] Here
is one hundred dollars expense money, and should you need
more we will send it to you, but a hundred dollars ought to
be sufficient. [*Hands money to* HERMAN.] Brown spends
too much money, and we don't want you to pattern after
him. You might as well walk from depots to hotels, unless
at night, and carry your baggage, it will be a saving of fifty
cents a day and perhaps more. So be off and let us hear
from you often, at least once a day. [ARMSTEAD and WAL-
TERS *bid* HERMAN *good-bye. Exit* HERMAN.] I will not be
surprised if McMillan offers Herman an interest in the business provided he sells a few bills of goods and makes a col-
lection or two. His address and smooth gramatical speech
should enable him to sell goods if nothing else were favorable. I remember now that I promised to be at home early
this evening. Mr. Armstead if you will be here until 4 o'clock
I will not remain longer.

Arm. Certainly, I will be here until 4 o'clock.

[*Exit* BAXTER.

Wal. Why is it that Mr. Baxter is always finding fault
with Mr. Brown?

Arm. I can't say as to that, complaint may be chronic in
his case, Mr. McMillan doesn't think much of his complain-

ing, or at least a person would judge so by his actions. When I was traveling for the house he found fault with every thing that I did; when I contracted large sales he found fault with the prices or the parties to whom I sold the goods. If I should happen to have a dull trip then he would complain and intimate that another man could be found who would sell more goods. I was under the impression that my sales ought to be satisfactory to the house. Mr. Brown always excelled me, and of late years has been selling as many goods as we both did during the time I traveled. It was Mr. McMillan's pleasure that I became a member of the firm, and not by any act or desire of Mr. Baxter, as he opposed it. Mr. Baxter became a member of the firm in the same way that I did, or in other words, he had no capital and it was at the pleasure of Mr. McMillan. Since receiving an interest in the business he has made considerable money, and, as he says, has married an heiress. He does not treat Mr. McMillan with the respect due him, for whatever Baxter's position now he owes it to the good offices of Mr. McMillan.

Wal. Have you examined Mr. Baxter's account within the last two months?

Arm. No, I seldom look at an account other than my own.

Wal. Within the last sixty days he has drawn twenty thousand dollars.

Arm. Twenty thousand dollars! That is quite a sum to take from the business at this time, and I must say that it looks unfavorable. The firm has made nothing during the year, and at its commencement Mr. Baxter's account was forty thousand dollars and my own was ten thousand dollars. I would like to mention the matter to Mr. McMillan but it would be unpleasant for me to do so.

[ARMSTEAD and WALTERS *resume their work. Curtain.*

ACT II.

SCENE I.—A Depot.—Herman's arrival.—Omnibus and Carriage
Drivers.

Drivers. Here's your omnibus for any part of the city!
Omnibus to any part of the city! Here's your carriage for
any part of the city! Carriage for the American House or
any other hotel in the city! [*Sees* HERMAN.] Kept on the
German plan.

Her. Vot vas ter biggest house in te city?

Driver. The Capital building is the largest.

Her. Vell I go dare.

Driver. Get right in! Here's your carriage for the Capital hotel of the city, or any other hotel or part of the city!
[*Departure of carriages and omnibuses. Curtain.*

SCENE II.—A Hotel Office.—Important Hotel Clerk.—Commercial Travelers in the Office.—Arrival of Herman.

Her. [*Addresses clerk.*] I vas gome to sday all night.

Clerk. Register your name. [HERMAN *registers.*] Your
room is No. 399. Have check for your baggage or have it
taken up?

Her. I leave him here vor a vile.

O'Neil. Sauerkraut will have a lofty sleep.

John. Yes, and a long run or a big jump in case of fire.

O'Neil. I wonder if Sauerkraut lies down when he goes
to bed or sleeps standing.

Cun. He will not want for sky-light, providing he rolls
the roof up a little, and can get plenty of fresh air by stick-
ing his head out of the window.

O'Neil. And sure you know the first peak that catches
the sunlight is crowned monarch of the hills, and sure
if Sauerkraut should roll the roof up a little or stick his
head out of the window, providing he finds the window to
be large enough, why should he not be a monarch as well
as a mountain? The highest pole knocks the persimmon,

and Sauerkraut will be the highest by the time he gets to 399, if he doesn't knock the persimmon already.   I like the cut of his coat, no doubt it is the latest style of the German Court.

John. Stop your remarks O'Neil, the man might hear you.

O'Neil. Perhaps it would be as well, I might be kicking at a bee with a splinter in its tail.

[HERMAN *approaches and addresses* CUNNINGHAM.

Her. Vas you vrom New York?

Cun. Yes, I am from New York,

Her. I vas vrom New York to-day.   Mr. Brown, you not know him, Mr. Brown vot travels vor sellin' dri goots?

Cun. Who! Charlie Brown that represents McMillan, Baxter & Armstead?

Her. Yes, dat vos him.   He pees on his bridal drip, and I vas gome to make a drip vor him.

Cun. I am well acquainted with Mr. Brown, and, if I mistake not, this is his friend Herman of whom I have heard him speak so often.

[CUNNINGHAM and HERMAN *shake hands.*

Her. Dat vos my name, Charles Frederick Herman Ulrich. [O'NEIL, JOHNSON and PEABODY *come up and are introduced.*

Cun. Gentlemen allow me to introduce to you Mr. Ulrich. He is making a trip for our old friend Brown, now on his bridal tour. [*All shake hands with* HERMAN.   MR. McFADDEN, *proprietor of the hotel, comes up and is introduced..*

Cun. Mr. McFadden, this is Mr. Ulrich, he represents McMillan, Baxter & Armstead, of New York, and is relieving Mr. Brown of business cares during his first month of connubial bliss.

McFad. [*Shakes hands with* HERMAN.] I am pleased to meet you Mr. Ulrich.   Mr. and Mrs. Brown spent a day with us last week. [*Addressing the party.*] We will try and take good care of Mr. Ulrich. [McFADDEN *goes to the register and addresses clerk.*] Have you given Mr. Ulrich a room?

Clerk. Yes, No. 399,

McFad. Change it to No. 24.

Clerk. Who! that Dutchman in 24?

McFad. Sir, he will occupy No. 24.

Her. Mr. McFadden ish der brobrietor of der hotel?

Cun. Yes, he is the proprietor and a clever gentleman.

Her. I dot der veller pehind dem diamonds vas brobrietor.

Pea. Mr. Ulrich, I have invited the gentlemen to spend the evening in my room, and as they have accepted the invitation I would be pleased to have you join us. Eight years ago I made my first tour as a commercial traveler, and during the trip formed Mr. Brown's acquaintance at this hotel, since then we have met often. Should he leave the road no doubt you will take his place, and if so, I hope we may be friends in the future, as Mr. Brown and I have been in the past. Several of us here have met this evening for the first time, but then it does not take commercial travelers long to become acquainted with each other. We are known at home; as men of the same profession we form acquaintances and friendships among ourselves; we form business acquaintances with those with whom we have business transactions; hotel proprietors treat us well, it being to their interest to do so; but otherwise we are a class distinct, we might say, from the balance of mankind. The newspapers remember us to the public as a herd of half educated drummers who are not at all necessary, and an injury to the commercial interests of the country.

O'Neil. And Peabody, I think you had better quit the business and become a member of one of the many distinguished Shaksperean clubs of the country, as a cackler you might make yourself entertaining to those unable to read. But if you do not like the higher drama, then I would advise you to take the stage for Woman's Rights, or go to writing epitaphs for country church yards. If you would stop drinking for a few days you might possibly get a job as a Temperance Lecturer at a good salary. You could tell what a hard case you have been without much reserve, as in the modern temperance field the devil and whiskey receive all the blame for bad actions, and the good people are not judged accountable for what they do. The harder you have been and the more whiskey you have drank the greater would be your pay, and should you engage in the business, your income would be equal to the gross earnings of a second class railroad. If we are going to your room let us go, or let us go to bed, I must be up by 9 o'clock in the morning.

Pea. Come on let us go to the room.

[*They all start,* O'NEIL *and* HERMAN *in the rear.*

O'Neil. Mr. Ulrich, it would be well to order your baggage sent to your room.

[HERMAN *orders baggage sent to room.*

O'Neil. Ven you go East or ven you go West, you stop at Reinhardt's dot vash de best.

Her. You know Sherman?

O'Neil. Nix verstay der hobdine velt de nominie schmockle. All I know about German is the beer part of it, and I like that very much. *Exit.* [*Curtain.*

SCENE III.—A Street Scene.

Enter BARNES *and* McLAIN *carrying valises.*

McLain. Barnes, I will go with you to Seth Longshore's place. Longshore sells groceries and liquors, and is good for all he will buy. I met a liquor man in his store once, but he failed to get an order. Longshore is from Jersey. If you should tell him that Jersey is your native state and praise him for keeping good liquors when he asks your opinion of an article of gin worth about one dollar a gallon for which he paid five, you will be sure to get an order. Liquor men who praise the gin sell him goods, but those who condemn it stand no chance whatever of making a sale.

Bar. Do you know what part of Jersey he came from?

McLain. He came from Trenton, and if any man is loyal to his native place, Longshore is. He believes Trenton to be the metropolis of the country, and Jersey the first State in the Union.

Bar. Can you go now?

McLain. Yes.

Bar. Let us go then. I will make a strong effort to sell him. [*Exit* BARNES *and* McLAIN. *Curtain.*

SCENE IV.—Longshore's Store.

Enter McLain *and* Barnes.

McLain. [*Shakes hands with* Longshore.] I am glad to find you at home. But then I never expect you to be absent, as I have always found you at your post. [*Introduces* Barnes.] Mr. Longshore, this is my friend Mr. Barnes. He is a Jerseyman and claims to sell good liquors. I told him you were a Jerseyman also, and if his liquors were not good that you would soon inform him of the fact.

Bar. [*Shakes hands with* Longshore.] I am glad to meet you Mr. Longshore. I always like to meet a Jerseyman, being from Jersey myself. Jerseymen are all gentlemen and good judges of liquor.

Long. I'm glad ye're come to see me, Mr. Barnes. Does me good now an' then have chance shake hands with Jerseyman, thar's nobody like 'em.

Bar. You think as I do, Mr. Longshore, men from other states may be good enough in their way, but they are not like Jerseymen; one Jerseyman is equal to a half a dozen of them; they blow and pipe about their states; and New Yorkers, Pennsylvanians and Ohioans have even gone so far as to try and make me believe their states were equal to Jersey. They might make a Vermonter or an ah— ah— spectacled Massachusetts chap believe such balderdash, but not a Jerseyman.

Long. Now ye're talkin' facts, Mr. Barnes, jist like Jerseymen talks. Lets have 'nother shake. [*They shake hands.*] Does me good shake hands with Jerseyman, ha ha ha! Buckeyes an' Yorkers tryin' fool Jerseyman what can't be fooled, ha ha ha. Them thar Mars'chusetts chaps, them thar Yorkers talkin' 'bout York state bein' bigger'n Jersey, ha ha ha ; them thar fellers have bin 'round this hur way too, blowin' thar pipes, Maryland oyster eaters, Nutmegers, Hoosiers, Hawkeyes, Buckeyes, Suckers, an' even Canucks brag-.gin' 'bout little Canada, ha ha ha. See Mr. Barnes ye're true Jerseyman. Lets have 'nother shake, [*They shake hands.*] ha ha ha.

Bar. What part of Jersey did you come from, Mr. Longshore?

Long. Me ! Why I'm from Trenton, what is a city.

Bar. Let us have another shake. [*They shake hands.*] I always like to meet a Jerseyman, but to meet a Jerseyman from my old native city, Trenton, is something that does me good.

Long. Ha ha ha, thar's no place like old Trenton. Old Trenton's thur place whar them thar Britishers and Hassins got what they didn't come fur. Them chaps didn't run 'ginst cow-boys when they come foolin' 'round old Trenton, that's what wus ther matter, ha ha ha !

Bar. You are right, Mr. Longshore, the British and Hessians could not stand the fire when Trenton boys done the shooting.

Long. Ye're right, Mr. Barnes, ye're not fiddlein' by air but by note, like Jerseymen fiddles.

Bar. Mr. Longshore, do you remember a family by the name of Vanskenk, that lived near the Post Office ?

Long. Vanskenk, Vanskenk. Yes, I b'lieve I remember them. What ever become of them thar gals ?

Bar. All married. Three of them live in the West, and two of them in Boston.

Long. Them thar wus all awful good lookin' gals, jist like Jersey gals is.

Bar. [*Opens sample case and looks at his watch.*] Mr. Longshore, I will now show you samples of our goods. Am sorry I haven't much longer to stay. The next time I come we will have a long talk.

Long. Next time ye come must stay hull day.

Bar. [*Takes samples from case.*] This, Mr. Longshore, is a sample of copper distilled rye, four years old, price three fifty per gallon; this is a sample of Jersey peach brandy, five years old, price six dollars ; this is a sample of Holland gin, price four fifty.

Long. [*Examines samples of brandy and gin.*] That's good brandy, that thar's Jersey brandy. That thar's tolerable gin too.

McLain. Don't let him cheat you, Mr. Longshore.

Long. 'Twas ye speakin ye'r self, was't Mr. McLain ?

and Mr. Longshore will order me out. We have a local wit down our way. Don't.

Long. Yes, thar's one uv them thar smart'n's here 'bouts what cum from over tother side uv Kansas post office, one uv them thar smart'n's known fur 'round as a hull ward, one uv them thar kind what the calves likes to chaw his coat, ha ha ha!

Enter MR. BOMBSHELL.

Bomb. [*Shakes hands with* LONGSHORE.] How are you to-day, Mr. Longshore?

Long. I'm well thank ye. [*Introduces* BOMBSHELL.] Boys this hur's Mr. Bombshell, uv ther firm uv Paycar & Bombshell, what sells teas.

Bomb. I am in very much of a hurry, Mr. Longshore. The gentlemen have more time than I have, and it will not take me long to show my samples. [*Opens sample case.*] I have a first Young Hyson that I must sell you. We have one half chest of it left. Let me look at some of your Young Hyson, if you have any.

Long. [*Points to package under counter.*] Thar it is in that thar chest. Tell me what ye think uv it.

Bomb. [*Goes to package and takes out tea, which he examines.*] Where did you get this tea?

Long. I got it uv a man what says he knows somethin' 'bout teas. That thar's Young Hyson, and cost eighty-five cents.

Bomb. [*Examining tea.*] This is not Young Hyson, it is Old Hyson, and not worth more than sixty cents. Who sent you such a tea as this for Young Hyson. I would like to know who would send you such a tea as this, and charge you eighty-five cents for it.

Long. Ye're right sure are ye, Mr. Bombshell, that he charged me too much fur it and that it arn't good.

Bomb. Yes, I am sure, and would like to know who cheated you.

Long. Mr. Bombshell, ye're the man what sent me that thar tea. I got that thar tea uv you, Mr. Bombshell.

Bomb. [*Goes back to package and takes more of the tea, which he examines.*] I see that I was mistaken, I took the first sample from the top and it happened to be broken leaves. I see now that the tea is much better than I thought it was, that it is a Young Hyson and a very good article. Let me show you a sample of a first Young Hyson. We have one half chest of it left.

Long. Ye're the man what sent me that thar Old Hyson fur Young Hyson, Mr. Bombshell. I don't want any uv yer tea to-day. Ye kin send a Jerseyman Old Hyson fur Young Hyson once, Mr. Bombshell, but yer can't do it agin. [BOMBSHELL *closes sample case and leaves the store.*

McLain. Bombshell no doubt will hereafter try and not explode prematurely and in his own camp.

Long. Bombshell can't send a Jerseyman Old Hyson fur Young Hyson an' then git a nuther chance to do it. Mr. Barnes, ye're showin' me samples uv yer goods, so I'll git yer 'pinion uv some gin what I've not bin out uv lately. [*Brings sample and hands it to* BARNES.] What say ye 'bout that thar gin?

Bar. [*Examines and tastes the gin.*] Well, I must say this is gin! Mr. Longshore, where did you get such an article of gin as this! Why, this is North Holland Gin, gin manufactured from juniper berries gathered from the Andes mountains of North Holland. No other man about here sells gin like this.

Long. See Mr. Barnes ye know somethin' 'bout liquors. Ha ha ha! one of them thar smart chaps was hur t'other day an' said that thar gin warn't worth dollar gallon, ha ha ha! lots uv them fellers don't know whar them thar Andoes mountains is. Am not much needin' goods, Mr. Barnes, but ye may send me one barrel uv this hur rye whiskey, and one barrel uv this hur Jersey brandy. Allers like to buy uv a man what understand his business.

Bar. [*Writes order in order-books.*] Am much obliged, Mr. Longshore, for the order.

Long. Send 'em 'long an' ye'll git yer money 'fore thirty days.

McLain. Mr. Longshore, what can I send you?

Long. Well, bins ye're travelin' in good company, ye may send me [McLAIN *writes order in order-book.*] one barrel A. sugar, one barrel Schneider crackers, one sack Rio coffee an' one keg soda. That's all.

McLain. Am much obliged, Mr. Longshore.

Long. Send 'em long an' ye'll git yer money 'fore thirty days.

Bar. Having other parties to see it will keep us busy to get through by evening, so we will have to bid you good-bye, Mr. Longshore. [*Reaches to shake hands.*

Long. Not yit. [*Brings brandy and glasses.*] Seldom drink any thing me self, an' not often ask any body else take drink, but we'll have little Jersey brandy 'fore ye go. [*Each one fills his glass.*

McLain. Here's health to all. [*Drinks.*

Long. An' here's to yer health, Mr. Barnes. An' yer health, Mr. McLain. An' that we'll prosper, and every body 'll prosper. And here's to ther flag an' the hull Union.

[*Drinks.*

Bar.
And here's to the land that we cherish and love,
That its flag may never be furled,
For a union of states, a union of hearts
And Liberty's march in the world :
To those who are true to their country and homes—
To the friends and scenes of their youth,
For of such we learn they are loyal and kind,
And strong in their friendship and truth ;
To the one who e'er sees in his backward gaze,
The bright streams of the years of yore,
Who remembers the joys of his earlier days ;
Here is health, long life to Seth Longshore.

[*Drinks.*

Long. Won't ye take somethin' more?

Bar. Not any I thank you, I have drank to my satisfaction, and if I should drink more it would be supurfluous.

McLain. Will you not drink again, Mr. Longshore, you did not drink much?

Long. No, I thank ye, I've drunk to my sanctificuscation, an' if I'd drink any more 'twould be flipus flopus. [BARNES and McLAIN *bid* LONGSHORE *good-bye.*   *Curtain.*

SCENE V.—Peabody's room at the hotel.—Johnson, O'Neil, Cunningham, Peabody and Herman sitting at a table.—A stand with wine bottles and goblets on it.

John. We have had a pleasant game. Mr. Ulrich always gets good cards and knows how to play them.

O'Neil. If he leads off in selling goods like he does in

seven-up he ought to continue on the road.   Peabody, ring
the bell for that shady son of the sunny clime of sunny
Africanus.   Let us have some wine.   When you have company, you should treat them well. [PEABODY *rings bell.*]
Mr. Ulrich, we have not done our share of the singing to-
night.

Pea. You have not done your share, and we expect both
of you to sing.   O'Neil you sing first, and then Mr. Ulrich
will sing.   [O'NEIL *sings.*

"There is not in this wide world a valley so sweet
  As that vale, in whose bosom the bright waters meet;
Oh! the last ray of feeling and life must depart
  Ere the bloom of that valley shall fade from my heart!

Sweet Vale of Avoca! how calm could I rest
  In thy bosom of shade, with the friends I love best;
Where the storms that we feel in this cold world should cease,
  And our hearts like the waters be mingled in peace."

Pea. Well done, O'Neil.   Now sing us a Scotch song, the
Scotch songs are the best.

O'Neil. My mother was a Scotch woman.   Would ye
moind thot now.

Pea. Then you ought to be able to sing Scotch songs.   If
it were not that your name is Irish, you would claim to be a
full blooded Scotchman.   You are the first Irishman I have
seen for some time who claims to be only half Scotch.   But
sing us a Scotch song, and you shall have the credit of being half Scotch.

O'Neil. Wad ye ha'e a half Scotch song?

Pea. No.   We want something old and all Scotch.

O'Neil. Somethin' auld an' a' Scotch.   [*Sings.*

"Come awa, hie awa,
  Come and be mine ain, lassie:
Row thee in my tartan plaid,
  An' fear nae wintry rain, lassie.

A bonny bower shall be thy hame,
  And drest in silken sheen, lassie:
Ye'll be the fairest in the ha',
  And gayest on the green, lassie.

Come awa, hie awa,
  Come and be mine ain, lassie:
Row the in my tartan plaid,
  An' fear nae wintry rain, lassie."

Pea. Well, what did the lassie say?

O'Neil. The lassie said:

Haud awa, bide awa,
  Haud awa frae me, Donald;
What care I for a' your wealth,
  And a' that ye can gie, Donald?

I wadna lea' my Lowland lad,
  For a' your gowd and gear, Donald;
Sae tak your plaid, an' o'er the hill,
  An' stay nae langer here, Donald.

Sae haud awa, bide awa,
  Come nae mair at e'en, Donald;
I wadna lea' my Lowland lad,
  To be a Highland queen, Donald."

Pea. That was a good half Scotch song. We believe your mother was a Scotch woman. [*Servant raps at the door.*

O'Neil. There's Hanibal Cæsar Pompey Ebenezer Snowball, let him in. [JOHNSON *opens door.*

Enter SERVANT.

Serv. Your orders gemmen.

O'Neil. And Snowball, you're a good fellow, bring us two bottles of wine to settle what you brought us before.
[*Exit Servant.*

John. Now, Mr. Ulrich, we will hear you sing.

Her. I bring my guitar, I get it. [*Exit* HERMAN.

Pea. Ulrich is crude, but there is good material in him.

O'Neil. Yes, all he wants is experience. No doubt he can sing like a tea-kettle.

Enter SERVANT *with wine.*

Serv. Wine, gemmen? [*Exit Servant.*

Pea. We will all take a drink. [*Pours out the wine.*

Enter HERMAN.

Her. I bring my guitar.

Pea. We will have some wine. [*All drink.*

O'Neil. Now we will hear Mr. Ulrich sing.

Her. Vot vill I zing?

O'Neil. Your favorite,

Her. My vavorite. I know vod dot pees. [*Plays and sings.*

"When the swallows homeward fly,
  When the roses scatter'd lie,
When from neither hill nor dale,
  Chants the silv'ry nightingale,
In these words my bleeding heart
  Would to thee its grief impart;
When I thus thy image lose,
  Can I, ah! can I e'er know repose.

When the white swan southward roves
To seek at noon the orange grove,
When the red tints of the west
Prove the sun is gone to rest,
In these words my bleeding heart
Would to thee its grief impart;
When I thus thy image lose.
Can I, ah! can I e'er know repose.

Hush my heart why thus complain,
Thou must too thy woes contain ;
Though on earth no more we rove
Loudly breathing vows of love,
Thou, my heart, must find relief;
Yielding to these words belief;
I shall see thy form again
Though to-day we part in pain."

[*Applauded by the company.*

Cun. I remember [*Looks at his watch.*] that my train leaves at 6 o'clock, and it is now 2 o'clock.

O'Neil. Yes, we must go, three hours sleep is not too much for generals like us.

Pea. We will drink the remaining bottle of wine.

O'Neil. Yes, we should not encourage intemperance by leaving it all for Peabody. Johnson will act as henchman, he can fill that office with more dignity and grace than any other one present. As a saloon keeper Johnson would be a success.

John. [*Pouring out wine.*

- Once more ere we part fill the goblets with wine :
  We were strangers well met at even ;
  Now each voice and each eye tells of friendship's tie,
  We are friends, not strangers at parting.

Her. Dot vas goot.   [*Each takes up a glass.*
Cun.

Each song has awakened some spell of the past.
And memory has lengthened the chain,
The joys that were ours has recalled them anew,
To gladden our spirits again.

Her. Dat vos besser as vos goot.
O'Neil.

So here's to the eve when as strangers we met,
The morn when as friends we are parting,
And here's to the night lent to story and song—
To mirth and our sorrows beguiling.

Her. Dot vos goot as vos besser as vas goot. [*All drink.*
CUNNINGHAM and O'NEIL *bid* PEABODY *good-bye,* JOHNSON and HERMAN *bid him good-evening. Exit   Curtain.*

SCENE VI.—A Village in the Mountains.—A Street Scene.

Enter McLAIN, CROSBY and ROSENBURG.

McLain. I've had a good trade, considering the excite-ment and talk about a fair count.

Cros. So have I.   A person can hardly believe that so much business is done in this mountain town.   Smithson told me that some of his customers come a distance of twen-ty miles.

Ros. Have either of you sold Cardoza ?

McLain. Not much, the old Indian never bought goods from a drummer.

Cun. Do you mean old Black Hawk ?

McLain. Yes, I never called to see him but once, and that done me.   Cardoza, they say, is one-fourth Indian, and for twenty years was connected with the army, as a scout.   It is said that he was one of the best scouts ever in the service of the government.   Nothing makes him so mad as to call him old Black Hawk.   When he wants goods he goes to the city, and will not buy from one of the boys.   We sell him, but one of the firm must wait on him.   When he was a scout no doubt he used to report to the Generals, and Indian like pre-fers doing business with the big chief.   Big Injun ! Chief ! Eat much hominy !

Ros. Well ! if there don't come Alf. Headley ! Wonder if he's selling goods ?

Cros. Yes, this is his first trip.   I met him yesterday.   He thinks he knows it all, and believes he is the best salesman on the road, and the finest looking man in the country.

McLain. Suppose we send him to sell old Black Hawk, and have some of the conceit taken out of him.

Cros. That will do, if he has not been to see him, we will have him go.

Enter HEADLEY.

Ros. [*Shakes hands.*] How ho you do, Mr. Headley, I understand you are drumming.   How do you find business ?

Head. O splendid ! splendid ?   All I want is a chance at a man, and if I don't sell him, he's not at home.

McLain. Have you sold Cardoza yet ?

Head. No. Where is his store? I hear that he is hard to sell, but I am going to sell him. Hard men to sell are the kind I like, they pay better.

McLain. They call Cardoza old Black Hawk. He used to be a government scout, and they say, the best on the border. He has been alone so much during his life that he is very fond of talking when he gets a chance, just like a modern temperance lecturer who has not had a drink for a long while, when he does get hold of a jug it takes all that's in it to fill him. It will be owing to how you introduce yourself, as to whether you sell him or not. You've got to be familiar. The way to waken him up, if you could do so, would be to step in unobserved, slap him on the back, and say, how are you old Black Hawk.

Head. I've been thinking of him, and that's about the way I thought of introducing myself. I" sell him, now you remember. Where's his store?

Cros. Just around the corner from the hotel.

Head. Well, I guess I will go and sell him.

[*Exit* HEADLEY.

McLain. Come on boys, we'll go and see Headley come out of the store with old Black Hawk after him.

Ros. Old Black Hawk might hurt him.

McLain. Of course he'd hurt him, but there' no danger of a coward like Headley getting hurt, he'll run at the first demonstration Black Hawk makes.

SCENE VII.—Cardoza's Store.

Cardoza. If I were younger and strong I would not be here. But years and wounds have done their work, and Cardoza the soldier and scout must seek a retreat, and no longer be known to the army and to fame.

[*Passes around counter to desk.*

Enter HEADLEY.

Head. [*Comes in unobserved—crosses room to desk and strikes* CARDOZA *on the back.*] How are you now, old Black Hawk?

Car. [*Angry and excited—reaches for something under the counter—does not find what he wants—looks around and does not see it.*] Tom! Where's the hatchet? [HEADLEY *becomes frightened and steps back from the counter.*] Tom! [CARDOZA *jumps over the counter.*] I'll teach you! [HEADLEY *drops his valise and hat, and starts for the door with* CARDOZA *in pursuit.* CARDOZA *returns and kicks valise and hat out of the door.*] That one got away, but the next one will not.   [*Curtain.*

SCENE VIII.—Office of a Village Hotel.

Enter HERMAN *carrying baggage.*

Her. [*Finds no one in the office—takes a view of the room.*] Dot vas vonies. Dem mans dole me dis vos der hodel, und ven I gomes no pody pees lookin' vor any pody vot vos hungry und vont a blace do schleab all night. Dot vas vonies. I gall dem, may pe do hear. [*Calls.*] Brobrietor! Dot vas vonies, all of dese dings mit oudt votchin who dake dem. Dere vos no goferment gollecdors und Injun Agents in dese barts of der goundry, or dese dings here pe nod sure dem vas safe. Dot vas vonies. I gall vor doze uder mans. [*Calls.*] Landlord! Bar-geeper!

Enter LANDLORD.

Land. I thought I heard some one calling. How do you do?

Her. I vos doin' pooty goot if I had somedings do eat und a blace all night do schleab.

Land. Yes, yes, we can accomodate you. Let me have your baggage. [*Takes* HERMAN'S *baggage.*] The train was a little late. They are eating supper now, and you can step right in.

Her. You lief here long?

Land. I have lived here nigh unto thirty years.

Her. You know Schorge Martin, who has a schtore here?

Land. Yes, I know George Martin. He is the biggest merchant in this section of the country and sells a power of goods.

Her. I stop off do zee Schorge Martin.

Land. There is no better man than George Martin in these parts. [*Opens door leading to dining-room.*] This is the way, step in to supper. [*Exit* HERMAN *and* LANDLORD.

Enter CROSBY, McLAIN, BARNES and ROSENBURG
from dining-room.

McLain. I wonder who that one hundred and sixty pounds of bologna is?

Bar. I don't know. Limburger may be a commercial footman or a sample slinger, one of the two no doubt. Rosenburg knows what a commercial footman is. He carried a four hundred pound pack for several years before reaching the rank of sample slinger.

Ros. Yez, I know.

Cros. Bologna, as you call him, will be in soon. Wait until you see more of him before you criticise too freely. I'm not much of a judge, but I think he has more good sense than either of you.

McLain. You may be right. We will wait. Boys, after a supper like that we ought to be able to sing some. [*Commences to sing and is joined by* ROSENBURG *and* BARNES.

CHORUS.—"When old Sim Simons is gone,
When old Sim Simons is gone;
Then young Sim Simons will be Sim Simons,
When old Sim Simons is gone." [REPEAT.

McLain. Crosby, you don't seem to be in very good spirits. Business not good?

Cros. I'm not in very good spirits, and as for business, there will not be much of that until the count is over. A man might get orders for Henry rifles if he had them—I believe that is the gun that shoots sixteen times and then repeats—but as to selling goods or making what we would call good sales that is out of the question. It is to be hoped that we will not have another such a count soon. I'm of the opinion that the American eagle is sick, and if the proper medicine is not administered that it will be several years before the count is over. The country is ready for a fight, and it will require but little to bring it on.

McLain. You are right, Crosby, the country is ready for a fight, I have commenced to feel revolutionary myself. I thought business might be dull with you or that you had received another of those letters from your firm on retrenchment and political economy.

Cros. As to the letters, they come regularly and pretty much after the style of the one I showed you. McCuen

puts in about one-third of his time looking over my expense
account, one-third in writing me to curtail my expenses, and
the remainder in eating and sleeping. He thinks a dollar a
day ought to be sufficient to pay my traveling expenses, and
knows no reason why business should not be good. McCuen
ought to be in Congress, we need two or three more wise
men there, men of broad and liberal views. He would at
once set about to have the army reduced in numbers and the
few remaining soldiers put on double duty and quarter ra-
tions. Retrenchment would be his motto, as long as it did
not reach his own pocket-book.

Enter HERMAN.

Her. Goot efenings, Shentlemans. [*All in one voice answer good-evening.*] Vos zome of yous a gommercial draveler, and knows Schorge Martin, vat geeps schtore in dese
down?

McLain. We are all salesmen and know George Martin.
He is the leading merchant of the place.

Her. I pees Charles Frederick Herman Ulrich, mit
McMillan, Baxter & Armstead, of New York, und stop of
do zee Schorge Martin.

Cros. I have heard Martin mention your firm, and speak
in the highest terms of George W. McMillan, the senior
partner. McMillan and Martin are old time friends; they
were class-mates at an institution of learning in Scotland.
McMillan is a Scotchman, and Martin was educated in Scotland.

Her. Schorge W. McMillan vas zo goot a mans as vas
any mans.

McLain. Mr. Ulrich, you don't believe a Scotchman to be
as good as a German, do you?

Her. You dink vat you dink. I dink a goot Scotchman
zo goot as vas a goot Sherman, and dot a goot Shermans
vas zo goot as pees any pody, let dems pe Americans, Eng-
lishmens or any podies else. You vas American und broud
of dat. I pees a Sherman man und broud of dat I am a
Sherman man. Dem Sherman mans vat pees not broud of
der Fatherland vas not right. [*Applauded by* CROSBY,
BARNES and ROSENBURG.

Bar. Mr. Ulrich, I believe as you do. Germans who ignore the virtues of the German government and people are not worthy of confidence or respect. Those who condemn the German civilization have no regard for industry, honesty, obedience, temperance, economy and education, and laws which respect alike the rich and the poor, the prince and the peasant.

Her. You zay somedings vos zo.

Cros. Mr. Ulrich, these are kind of war times. We know our national hymns and war songs, but they do not answer in the present crisis. We undertake to sing them but find that instead of enthusing they invariably bring on sick headache or cholic. Sing us a German war song, we believe our American hymns to be the best, but they are not appropriate to the present war feeling.

Her. I zing a Sherman war zong. [*Sings.*

"A roar like thunder strikes the ear,
  Like clang of arms or breakers near,
"On for the Rhine, the German Rhine!"
  "Who shields thee, my beloved Rhine?"
Dear Fatherland, thou need'st not fear—
  Thy Rhineland watch stands firmly here.

A hundred thousand hearts beat high,
  The flash darts forth from ev'ry eye,
For Teutons brave, inured by toil,
  Protect their country's holy soil.
Dear Fatherland, thou need'st not fear—
  Thy Rhineland watch stands firmly here.

The heart may break in agony,
  Yet Frenchman thou shalt never be,
In water rich is Rhine; thy flood,
  Germania, rich in heroes' blood.
Dear Fatherland, thou need'st not fear—
  Thy Rhineland watch stands firmly here.

When heavenward ascends the eye,
  Our heroes' ghosts look down from high :
We swear to guard our dear bequest,
  And shield it with the German breast.
Dear Fatherland, thou need'st not fear—
  Thy Rhineland watch stands firmly here.

As long as German blood still glows,
  The German sword strikes mighty blows,
And German marksmen take their stand,
  No foe shall tread our native land.
Dear Fatherland, thou need'st not fear—
  Thy Rhineland watch stands firmly here.

We take the pledge. The stream runs by,
  Our banners, proud, are waiting high,
On for the Rhine, the German Rhine !
  We all die for our native Rhine,
Hence, Fatherland, be of good cheer—
  Thy Rhineland watch stands firmly here."

McLain. By the way, Crosby, have you sold Mike Bonham?

Cros. No, nor you haven't either. Mike Bonham never bought goods of a commercial traveler ; if he wanted a box of crackers he'd go to New York for them before he'd give the order to a salesman. He pays ten per cent more for his goods than any other man in the place but hasn't found it out yet.

McLain. I never sold him and never knew of a drummer selling him. For a little fun how would it do to make a run on him this evening ? You to go in first with your cracker samples and try to force a sale ; when you come out Rosenburg will take your samples and try him, and then Barnes, Mr. Ulrich and myself will each give him a call. He'll not know that the samples are the same. When five of us concentrate on one article we may be able to make a breach in the old cuss' cussedness. We will represent ourselves to be from different cities, but will all make the same speech. What do you say, Crosby ?

Cros. I'm willing, I'm ready for anything from a foot race to a revolution.

Ros. He deserves it vrom vot I've heard, and let us give it to him.

Bar. Yes, let us play it. Get your sample-case, Crosby, and we will go. Mr. Ulrich will go with us. [CROSBY *gets sample-case.*

Her. Yes, I gares vor a leedle vones doo.

[*All leave the office. Curtain.*

SCENE IX.—A Village Store.—Several men and boys in the Store.—Michael Bonham, proprietor, behind desk at the end of counter.

Enter CROSBY.

Cros. Is this Michael Bonham's store ?

Men and boys. [*Pointing to desk, and in one voice.*] This is Michael Bonham's store. He's behind the desk.

[BONHAM *comes from behind desk.*

Cros. [*Hands card and shakes hands.*] This is Mr. Bonham, I believe ?

Bon. Bonham is my name.

Cros. I am glad to see you, Mr. Bonham. My name is McBride, I represent Bruce, Wallace, Montrose & Co., formerly of Glasgow, Scotland, now of Boston, manufacturers of crackers. [*Opens sample-case and spreads out samples.*] I want to show you a few samples of our crackers and give you an opportunity to buy good crackers at low prices.

Bon. No doubt you have good goods, but then I do not wish to buy just at this time. You may leave your card, and when I come down I will call.

Cros. Mr. Bonham, you may think you do not wish to purchase at this time, but when you have examined the samples and learned the prices of our crackers, you will not fail to give me an order. [*Takes from his pocket a large price list, which he unrolls.*] This is a list of the names and prices of the different grades and kinds of crackers we manufacture, and when you have looked at the samples and examined the list closely you will not fail to give me an order.

Bon. Yes, but ——

Cros. Yes, our cracker establishment is not only the largest cracker establishment in this or any other country, but our capacity for making crackers is greater than the capacity of any other cracker manufactory. We make a greater variety of crackers, crackers superior in quality and style to all other crackers, crackers warranted to be free from mould or breakage, every cracker warranted to be all cracker, and ——

Bon. Yes, but ——

Cros. Yes, I knew you would say so, and not fail to give me an order.

Bon. Yes, but ——

Cros. Yes, if only for ten boxes of our lemon crackers or fifty boxes assorted of our water crackers, soda crackers, ginger crackers, celebrated cider crackers, oyster crackers, best ever made cream crackers, never before equaled butter crackers, sweetest ever known sugar crackers, liberty crackers, fire crackers or any other kind or style of our extensive line of crackers ——

Bon. Yes, yes, but ——

Cros. Yes, all we wish to have you do at this time is to

try a few boxes of our crackers. [*Holds up samples.*] This is
our celebrated liberty cracker, at the present time we manufacture them only for the Cuban insurgents and South American republics, but if our political troubles should not be
settled, then we will manufacture no other cracker, and will
use our whole factory in making the liberty cracker, and
brand them, fair count crackers.

Bon. I will wait 'till I come down.

Cros. [*Puts samples in case.*] I am sorry, Mr. Bonham,
that I am unable to sell you at this time. [*Shows price list.*]
Will you not look over our price list.

Bon. Not now, I will wait 'till I come down.

Cros. [*Closes sample-case and folds price list.*] Well, then
I will bid you good-bye, [*Shakes hands.*] hoping that you
will be down soon.   [*Exit* CROSBY.

Enter ROSENBURG.

Ros. Is dis Michael Bonham's store?

Men and boys. [*Pointing to desk, and in one voice.*] This
is Michael Bonham's store.   He's behind the desk.

                    [BONHAM *comes from behind desk.*

Ros. Dis is Mr. Bonham, I pelieve?

Bon. Bonham is my name.

Ros. [*Hands card and shakes hands.*] I am zo happy to
zee you, Mr. Bonham. My name is Vanderdecken Heimen-
schlimmer, I represent Bismarck, Moltke, Schiller & Co.,
vormerly of Berlin, Prussia, now of St. Louis, United States,
America, manufacturers of crackers. [*Opens valise and
spreads out samples.*] I shust want to show you zome nice
zamples of crackers, and give you shust one shance to buy
a bill of crackers lower den I zell any pody else, sheaper den
I zell a bruder.

Bon. Yes, no doubt, but I have a full stock and I do not
wish to buy.   You may leave your card and when I come
down I will call.

Ros. I would like zo well to give you shust one shance to
buy sheap.   I zell all der big houses, and ven I gome back
dey all zay I vas der man vat zells such sheap crackers, and
der band blays.

Bon. Yes, but ——

Ros. Yes, you shust look at zo nice crackers, and how sheap. Our cracker establishment ish ter biggist cracker establishment vot was ever in dis or any uder country what was ever known.

Bon. I do not wish to buy now. When I come down I will call.

Ros. You better dake twenty boxes of our zelebrated sugar crackers, twice as zweet as sugar, or twenty boxes of lemon crackers, twice as zweet as lemons. We make all der kind of crackers what is made. Oyster crackers, twice as good as oysters; gream crackers, twice as nice as gream; butter crackers, twice as good as butter; water crackers, twice as good as water; soda crackers, christmas crackers or any uder cracker what was ever made.

Bon. I do not want any.

Ros. You dink you not buy, but shust zee how sheap. [*Spreads out an extensive price list.*] Shust look, ven you read ter brice list all over. [BONHAM *turns away.*[You not want sheap crackers? [*Puts samples in case and folds up price list.*] I'm zo zorry you not want to buy zo good crackers, and zo sheap.	[BONHAM *returns.*

Bon. I do not wish to buy now, I will call when I come down.

Ros. I now bid you good-bye. You lose a pargain.
	[*Exit* ROSENBURG.

Enter McLAIN.

McLain. Is this Michael Bonham's store?

Men and boys. [*Laugh, and in one voice pointing to desk.*] This is where he stays. He's behind the desk.

Bon. Who is it that wishes to see Michael Bonham?

McLain. Mr. Bonham, if you are not too busily ingaged, I would be pleased to see you. [BONHAM *comes from behind desk.* McLAIN *shakes hands with him.*] I am glad to meet you, Mr. Bonham. [*Presents card which is refused by* BONHAM *and falls on the counter.*] My name is Rufus Falstaff, I represent Blackstone, Coke, Erskine & Co., formerly of London, England, now of New York, manufacturers of crackers. [*Opens sample-case and spreads out samples.*

Bon. I am not in want of crackers, sir.

[*Men and boys laugh.*

McLain. Mr. Bonham, you may think you do not wish to purchase, but ——

Bon. I mean what I say, sir. You can put up your samples.

McLain. [*Takes price list from his pocket and unrolls it.*] No doubt, Mr. Bonham, you ——

Bon. [*Excited*] Sir, I know my own business better than you can tell me. There have been two cracker men here this evening before you.

McLain. They received your orders then?

Bon. No.

McLain. I am glad. [*Spreads out samples.*] When you examine our samples of crackers and have learned our prices you will not fail to give me an order. [BONHAM *stands and listens, men and boys laugh.*] Our cracker establishment is not only the largest cracker manufactory in the world, but as far as we know, it is a much larger cracker establishment than is to be found upon any other one of the planets of the solar systems within the light of the grand central sun of the universe; not only this, but we manufacture more kinds of crackers, and better crackers, crackers superior in every respect to crackers made by other cracker establishments. [*Takes up a sample.*] I would like to take your order for five hundred boxes of this make of crackers, our highly flavored and superior lemon crackers, or an order for a few thousand boxes assorted of our celebrated oyster crackers, soda crackers, cider crackers, sailor crackers, cinnamon crackers, corn crackers, butter crackers, Boston crackers, sugar crackers, medicated crackers ——

Bon. That will do young man, that is enough.

McLain. Yes, but we have many other kinds of crackers. We have the celebrated liberty cracker, which is pressed, baked and air dried, and warranted to stand either cold or heat, rain or fog. At this time we manufacture them only for North pole expeditions, Mexican patriots, Cuban insurgents and South American republics, but ——

Bon. That will do, you may put up your crackers.

McLain. [*Puts crackers in case and takes up price list.*] Will you not look over our price list, Mr. Bonham, I may have missed the name of the cracker you want?

Bon. No.

McLain. [*Closes sample-case and folds price list.*] Am sorry, Mr. Bonham, that I cannot sell you a bill of crackers. When you come down call and see us. I will now bid you good-bye, Mr. Bonham. [*Offers to shake hands but is refused.*] Good-bye, Mr. Bonham. [*Exit* McLain.

Bon. I want no more of this, I will have no more of it, I will have nothing to do with drummers.

[*Goes behind desk.*

Enter HERMAN.

Her. Pees dese der blace vere Michael Bonham geeps a schtore?

Men and boys. [*In one voice pointing to desk.*] This is the place. He's behind the desk.

Her. I veel zo glad, does mans dell me eif I go here dese vas der blace, und I gome do zee Michael Bonham. [BON- HAM *comes from behind desk.*

Bon. My name is Bonham.

Her. [*Shakes hands with* BONHAM.] I veel zo glad vot I meet Michael Bonham [*Hands* BONHAM *a card which he receives but does not read*] und my name vas Shacob Schummelbacher. [BONHAM *walks away, men and boys laugh.*] You gome back ven I dole you vot I vas. [BONHAM *returns.*

Bon. What do you say, sir?

Her. I zay you dink nudings right vor a vile ven you dink eif I vas der Shacob vat blay dot drick vile der old shentlemen gouldn't zee him a leedle, do know vor sure eif it vas Esau. [*Boys cry more crackers.*] I vas not der Shacob vot sheat Esau his bruder, und gome do sheat you. I vos Shacob Schummelbacher mit der Liberdy gracker vorks.

Men and boys. That's the cracker house.

Her. [*Addresses bystanders.*] You zay now zomeding zo. [BONHAM *walks away.*] You gome back ven I dole you zomedings an' make no voolishness. [BONHAM *returns.*

Bon. What do you say, sir? I want none of your crackers.

Her. You vont zomedings ven I geif you do hear aboud does Liberdy grackers, und dole you don't got vot make you rich. [*Opens sample-case.*] You ton't dink der Liberdy gracker vorks vas bigger und better as vas all do gedder of gracker vorks peside. You don't vould dink undil I dole you, we gief avay vor nudings does gommon grackers und sharge only vor Liberdy grackers. [*Spreads out samples.*] Does vas grackers I zend you vor nudings.

Men and boys. Show your Liberty crackers, the crackers you are showing are worth nothing.

Her. [*Addressing men and boys.*] You zay two dimes zomedings zo. [*Spreads out samples of Liberty crackers. BONHAM stands and listens.*] Does leedle vellers I zell you now, und you den order dese big vones ven you hafe dried der leedle vones. You eat der Liberdy gracker und you got schmart dot you know vat liberdy vas, und hafe de right do zell dree quarts vor a gallon, und dirteen ounces vor a pound, und dot money is vat makes der mules go. Dose big bolerditions eat dem Liberdy grackers und know liberdy vas der right big dings vor dem. Does railroad mens eat der Liberdy grackers und know liberdy pees der right do buy dem law-makers do make laws vat dey vont. Dem legisladors eat Liberdy grackers an' know dey hafe der right do zell der votes. Dem bank an' insurance shentlemens eat Liberdy grackers und know zomeding vot liberdy vas.

Men and boys. Them's the crackers, them's the Liberty crackers.

Her. [*Addresses men and boys.*] You zay dree dimes zomedings zo. I zend you zome Liberdy grackers, und ven you got rich der Flunky Digers call der names der Bonham Digers, und do or dree days pevore der ball you hear dose drum beat, der beobles sheer, und all of does dwendy-vive Digers march droo der city, an' you pees galled Colonel, vich vos gome do mean cock of der valk, vich vas gookedoodle. Den ven you vas a gookedoodle you zoon gots do be a Sheneral, vich vas got do mean every dings an' nudings in bardickular.

Bystanders. Them's the kind of soldiers. We want no regular army.

Her. [*addressing men and boys.*] You zay vour dimes zcmedings zo.

Bon. We want no more of this.

Her. You not buy Liberdy grackers.

[*Puts sample in case.*

Bon. I will have no more of this, put up your samples and go.   I have nothing to do with drummers.

[*Goes behind desk.*

Her. I go ven a mans dole me dat vor sure.

[*Exit* HERMAN.

Enter BARNES.

Bar. Is this Michael Bonham's store ?

Men and boys. [*Laugh, and in one voice pointing to desk.*] This is the place.   He's behind the desk.

Bon. Who now wishes to see Bonham ?

Bar. If not too busily engaged, Mr. Bonham, I would like to see you for a few moments. [BONHAM *comes from behind desk.*   BARNES *reaches to shake hands but is refused.*   Am glad to see you, Mr. Bonham.

Bon. You are ?

Bar. Yes, very glad to meet you.   My name ——

Bon. It is ?

Bar. Yes, my name is Eugene Jarvis, I represent ——

Bon. [*Excited.*] You do, do you ?

Bar. Yes, I represent McMahon, Beauharnais, Murat & Co., late of Paris, France, now of Philadelphia, manufacturers of crackers. [*Opens sample-case.*] I want to show you samples of our crackers.

Bon. [*Angry and excited.*] You do? I will have no more of this. [*Turns and calls.*] Bob! Do you hear me ? Bob ! [*Walks backward and forward behind the counter.*]   I will have no more of this.   Bob ! [*Boy comes to the door.*] Put out the lights—put up the lights and put out the shutters ! [*Boy blows out a light.*] Crackers, crackers, the whole d—d country has gone into the cracker business ! [BARNES, *men and boys crow'd to the door, crying crackers, crackers.*

[*Curtain.*

ACT III

SCENE I.—Office of McMillan, Raxter & Armstead.—Armstead and Walters in the office.

Enter BAXTER.

Bax. [*Excitedly.*] Wise & Morton have failed; we hold their paper for fifty thousand dollars, which falls due on Friday. It is said they will pay little or nothing, having lost heavily in a grain speculation, and no doubt worth nothing at the best. Brown contracted the debt, and a man that would sell such parties should be discharged from the service of any commercial house. He has been absent almost a month and not heard from. Our obligations for one hundred and fifty thousand dollars matures in one week from to-day, and a few more failures will bankrupt the firm.

Enter McMILLAN.

McMil. Good-morning, gentlemen.
Bax. Wise & Morton have failed; their note for fifty thousand dollars falls due on Friday.
McMil. Is it possible! These failures are becoming alarmingly frequent! One hundred and five thousand in one week is very severe. Our note for one hundred and fifty thousand will be due one week from to-day. With this last failure we will not have money sufficient to meet it. I disposed of some stock a few days since, and have seventy-five thousand on call in the Fidelity Savings Bank. The firm can have the use of the money for a time, which will enable us to meet our obligations. Were it not that I happen to have the money on call we could not well meet our note. But our obligations must be met as long as I have money to meet them. Have we no word from Mr. Brown?
Bax. No, I think he has gone to Europe or South America, and will return in the Spring.
McMil. Have we heard from Herman within the last few days? He is doing well, even better than I expected.
Bax. We have not heard from him since last Friday. At first he wrote every day, then every two days, and lately,

every four days. We have not heard from him to-day, so I
suppose he has lengthened the time to eight days.

McMil. When will Banks & Weddel's note be due ?

Bax. It was due on Saturday. We should have a return
to-day, and not later than to-morrow.

Enter BANK MESSENGER.

Bax. Well ! what now?

Mess. Banks & Weddel's note—have made an assign-
ment.   [*Exit messenger.*

McMil. Can it be possible ! Have made an assignment !
Why Mr. Brown received from them a statement of their
affairs, and Banks represented the firm to be worth one hundred thousand dollars. They obtained the goods under
false pretense, and should be made to suffer for it. Send
their note to Herman at once, with all necessary instructions.
Have him see our attorney, Mr. Carrick, and if they do not
pay the amount we will have them prosecuted without de-
lay. To obtain goods under false pretense is a penitentiary
offense, and we should not be wanting in effort to bring them
to justice. Instruct Herman to accept of no compromise.
Mr. Armstead lose no time in attending to the matter, tele-
graph him to wait, the papers will reach him by Friday.
Mr. Brown's estimate of the character of the men was cor-
rect. [BAXTER *leaves the office.*] There was a time when I
judged no man of dishonesty, in fact I believed all men to
be honest, men were more honest than now. There was a
time when positions of honor were filled by honorable men,
men who guarded the interests of the people and sought the
welfare of their country. To-day, all men are not dishonor-
able, but it seems that a want of integrity is pervading every
avenue of public and civil life, and that pretense and intrigue
have more than equaled worth and honesty in the race for
public and civil precedent. [*Turns to* WALTERS] What
amount of money have we in bank?

Wal. [*Refers to check-book.*] The firm has in bank a
credit balance of seventy-five thousand dollars, there are
four notes, on good firms, amounting to thirty thousand
dollars, which will be paid during the week. By Saturday
the firm will have a credit balance of one hundred and five
thousand dollars.

Arm. Mr. Walters, you will find a check in the drawer for four thousand dollars. which please give me credit for and deposit.

McMil. We are much obliged, Mr. Armstead. For the first time we are in need of money, and four thousand dollars will be an addition to what we have. By Saturday, including your check, we will have one hundred and nine thousand dollars, and on Friday or Saturday I will give the firm a check for the seventy-five thousand I have on deposit in the Fidelity Savings Bank, which will increase our credit balance to one hundred and eighty thousand dollars. I was under the impression that we had more money.

Wal. Mr. Baxter has drawn some money during the last few days.

McMil. Has he drawn much?

Wal. Twenty thousand dollars.

McMil. Is it possible! He has not been making investments that I have heard of, and twenty thousand dollars at this time, when so many of our customers are failing and we are in need of money, is quite a sum to take from the business. I have not felt well this morning and think perhaps it would be best for me to go home and rest during the remainder of the day.   [*Exit* McMILLAN. *Curtain.*

SCENE II.—Office of Banks & Weddel.—Banks in the office.

Enter WEDDEL.

Wed. Banks, you should have had more sense than to have given McMillan, Baxter & Armstead that statement of our affairs. It may give us some trouble. From the rest of our creditors we have nothing to fear, they must take what we see proper to give them and be satisfied with what they get. I spoke to Roby in relation to the matter and he thinks you made a mistake, that it would have been better not to have bought the goods, and that our only course, providing they have the statement, will be to pay them in full.

Enter ROBY, *attorney for* BANKS & WEDDEL.

Roby. And how are you now?

Banks. All well.

Wed. I was mentioning the conversation we had.

Roby. Yes, well the only safe course to pursue will be to pay the note and try and get the statement.

Banks. If you could arrange the matter for us we would be willing to pay you three thousand dollars additional.

Roby. It would be impossible for me to do so. My only advice is to pay the note and get the statement, any other course will lead you into trouble.

Enter HERMAN and CARRICK, *attorney.*

Her. Vas dis der office vere Banks & Veddel vos geepin'?

Banks. This is their office. My name is Banks, [*Pointing to* WEDDEL.] and that is Mr. Weddel. Any thing we can do for you?

Her. I gome vrom McMillan, Baxter & Armstead, of New York. I gome vor no voolishness, but gome vor dwenty-vive tousand dollar vot you owe. [*Produces note.*] Dis vas your note and it must be baid right now. You make voolishnesss mit compromise or bromise, I hear nuding. I vas gome vor der money right now. You not bay it I pring te constable, I prings ter bolice, I prings der sheriff and have you taken vor robbers, vor valse bretense. [*Produces statement.*] You sign him dot you vas wort one hundred tousand dollars, and pies dwenty-vive tousand dollar wort of goots, now you vas broke up, vich vas a lie, and I make no voolishness. You not bay him you vill be arrested vor robbers.

Wed. [*Shakes hands with* HERMAN.] Of course we will pay the amount. We are glad to see you. The debt was contracted before our embarrassment and we have left money in trust to meet our note in favor of McMillan, Baxter & Armstead. If you have the note and the statement of our financial condition at the time it was given we will take them and give you the money. You do us a kindness in presenting the note, it will save us the trouble of remitting. Shall we give you a draft, or would you prefer the currency?

Her. I vont der money in greenpacks, dem vas goot.

Wed. [*Pointing to* ROBY.] Our attorney and Mr. Banks will go for the money and have it here in a few minutes. Your name?　　　　　[*Exit* BANKS and ROBY.

Her. My name vas Charles Frederick Herman Ulrich, gommercial draveler, peesnis agent and lawyer vor McMillan, Baxter & Armstead, of New York.

Wed. Yes, yes. Be seated, the gentlemen will return in a few moments. I suppose your friend is from New York, also?

Her. No, he vas vrom Cincinnati.

Car. I came with Mr. Ulrich he being unacquainted with the locality of your office.

Wed. It is a sore trial for those who have labored for many years to accumulate wealth, and when success has been attained to see all swept away by an unwise speculation. Dishonest men will defraud their creditors and retain money which does not belong to them, but Banks & Weddel could not do as much As christian gentlemen, and unforgetful of their high social standing and their relations to the church, they can but set an example of faith and honesty to the world.

Enter BANKS and ROBY.

Banks. We have the money, the gentlemen will please count it.

[HERMAN and CARRICK *receive and count the money.*

Car. Twenty-five thousand dollars, the amount wanted. Mr. Ulrich you will now give the note to them. [HERMAN *hands note to* WEDDEL.] If not objectionable I would like to retain the statement given by Banks & Weddel to McMillan, Baxter & Armstead. My name is Carrick, and as I am employed by the creditors of Banks & Weddel I would be pleased to retain the statement,

Banks. [*Excitedly.*] You cannot have it.

Car. Just as you like, I have a duplicate of it, which can be proven to be a genuine copy of the original. [*Addresses* HERMAN.] Mr. Ulrich, we will go to the Express office. You wish to remit the money.

Her. We go. [*Turns and addresses* BANKS and WEDDEL.] It vas vell enough dat you baid der money.

[*Exit* HERMAN and CARRICK.

Wed. And that was Carrick the collector! We have the statement given by us to McMillan, Baxter & Armstead, but

Carrick has a copy of it, and can produce evidence to prove that it is a true one, which will expose our duplicity and rascality to the world. There is but one course left us, and that is to see Carrick, and try and have to-day's transactions kept a secret. I have but little hope of the result. We have served the devil in Heaven's livery, but we may be forced to serve him in his own livery. [*All are excited.*] Come, let us go at once. [*Curtain.*

SCENE III.—Office of McMillan, Baxter & Armstead.

Enter BAXTER.

Bax. [*Looks at his watch.*] I am early ; plenty of time ; a half hour before either of them will be here. Yes, yes, I will draw a check for forty thousand dollars, and be at the bank when it opens. [*Takes check-book from safe and draws check.*] That will do. Pay to Aaron Baxter or order, forty thousand dollars, McMillan, Baxter & Armstead. Money is what we want ; money is what we must have if we would be anything in the eyes of the world. Money is the standard and the only true measure by which to judge man or woman. Money gives us character and social and political standing, all of which it should do. Talent, honesty, bravery, ha! ha! ha! foolish sounding words, well enough they may be when backed by money, but contemptible without it. Philanthropy, an empty sound; poverty, the reward of honest fools. On Tuesday next the firm of McMillan, Baxter & Armstead will close its doors,—will be compelled to make an assignment for the benefit of its creditors. The other members of the firm may give what they have in foolish acts of honesty, but Aaron Baxter will not sink to the level of the rabble, he will not sacrifice his standing in the eyes of the world in the name of honesty. Others may do as they choose, McMillan and Armstead may give what they have, but they and their giving will soon be forgotten, and the time will come when they will praise the wisdom and court the favor of Aaron Baxter. Money should be the sole object, and that which prompts a man to act. We live in an age of reason, and our acts should be guided by reason. I married for money, ha! ha! ha! When my honora-

ble father-in-law takes his departure, ha! ha! ha! the time
will come when Aaron Baxter will be a man among men,
and beggars shall feel his power and know his worth, [*Looks
at his watch*.] The bank will soon open, I must go.

[*Exit* BAXTER.

Enter ARMSTEAD and WALTERS.

Arm. It seems that no one suspected the true condition
of the Fidelity Savings Bank until within the last two days.
Depositors will loose their deposits in full.   Mr. McMillan
will loose seventy-five thousand dollars. I am sorry, not only as to the effect his loss will have on the firm, but that
such a man should suffer by the acts of rascals.   The den
of hypocrites and thieves would have been a more appropriate name than the Fidelity Savings Bank.   Owing to
Mr. McMillan's loss we may not be able to meet our note
which falls due on Monday.   Heretofore, his paper would
have been gladly received for three times the amount we
need, but it is known that we have lost heavily of late, and
a further loss of seventy-five thousand dollars I fear will
prevent him from getting the money.   He may have friends
who will come to his rescue, or at least there are those who
should do so if they would do for him what he has done for
them; I have little hope however.   The vice of ingratitude
is the inherent vice of the hog, but it is also prevalent
among men, and tact and hypocrisy are too often mistaken
for friendship,

Enter McMILLAN.

McMil. It would seem that misfortunes, like birds, come
in flocks.   By the failure of the Fidelity Savings bank I lose
seventy-five thousand dollars, and am unable to render the
firm further assistance, I would gladly do so but I have no
money.   We need forty thousand dollars.   Any banking
house would be secure in discounting our paper for three
times the amount, but to-day I have no credit and no friends.
Men, for whom I endorsed and rendered aid when they
most needed support, shun me, and those who owe their
prosperity to my good offices do not know me now.   To-
day I have learned more than I knew in the past; I have
learned that when fortune favors us selfishness, transgression

and ingratitude seek us in the guise of friendship, but shun us in the hour of adversity. There is a moral heroism, as well as a heroism in war. Many a craven heart is sheltered by the cloak of wealth, and until the hour of battle bravery is attributed to many a coward. Self denial, sincerity and truth are attributes which the craven does not possess, and bravery is prompted by impulses which the coward never feels; they are not possessed only by those in a certain sphere of life they belong alike to the rich and the poor, and those who possess them are the true noblemen of the land. Our losses have been exagerated, we are unable to meet our obligations and we must make an assignment. Has Mr. Baxter been here to-day?

Wal. [*Examining check-book.*] It would seem so. He has drawn a check of this date for forty thousand dollars, in favor of Aaron Baxter.

McMil. Do I understand you! has drawn a check for forty thousand dollars! He had already drawn as much as his interest in the business. And is Aaron Baxter too a rascal! And am I to receive ingratitude and theft at the hands of Aaron Baxter! I am unwell and must go home. Please go to the bank, and when you have learned the particulars come and tell me.   [*Exit* McMillan.

Arm. [*Addressing* WALTERS.] Bring the check-book.
          [*Exit* ARMSTEAD and WALTERS. *Curtain.*

SCENE IV.—Washington City.—A Street Scene.

Enter HERMAN, *carrying valise.*

Her. I bass along by dat vine house and dot vine poody lady vot vas dustin' der vinders, dot vine poody girl I dot vas Louisa. She look at me, I look at her, den der vine lady vot vos own ter house call her avay. Dat vos Louisa ; it cannot vas bossible dat vos not Louisa. I go pack and know ver sure.   [*Exit* HERMAN.

Enter LOUISA, *carrying basket.*

Lou. I not meet him. I gome round der street zo vast, but he has vent by. I dink dat vos Herman Ulrich, and hurry zo vast. Dot schmile vas zo like Herman used to

laugh.   But Herman vent to New York, and I gome to Baltimore.   He care not vor Louisa now.   Herman vas a man and vear goot clothes, and marry one rich lady.   Louisa work vive year and make two hundred dollar vat she save. Herman vas a man and marry one rich lady.
                              [*Sees* HERMAN *coming and steps aside.*

                              Enter HERMAN.

Her. She vas gone already.   [*Sees* LOUISA.   Dat vos Louisa, I know vor sure.   [*Stops and then approaches.*] Dis vos my Louisa dat I hunt zo long.
Lou. You vas Herman who I wait vor zo long.
                              [*They greet each other.*
Her. Herman vos not vorgot Louisa. [*Takes her basket and picks up his valise.*] I go home vid you, and you go my vife to New York.   I vas a gommercial draveler now, and peesnis agent and lawyer vrom New York, but vas not vorgot Louisa vor any pody else.   [*Exit.*

                  Enter POLICEMAN and CITIZEN.

Cit. He was on this street twenty minutes ago, and I don't think has passed up this far.
Pol. You are sure that he is selling goods without a license ?
Cit. Yes, I am sure, when I asked him he told me that he would attend to his own business.   He's as Dutch as cabbage.   You needn't be afraid, I will give you half of what I get, which will be half of the fine.   You must take him before old Thomas Jefferson Wise, he'll make the fine heavy, which will be all the better for us.

                        Enter HERMAN.

Cit. [*Pointing to* HERMAN.] That is the man.
Pol. [*Stops* HERMAN.]You are selling goods are you not?
Her. You vant to buy zome goots ?
Pol. Show me your license.
Her. Vot you ask me vor license, I vas not gome here vor votin'.
Pol. You are selling goods without a license, and you are my prisoner.   [*Takes hold of* HERMAN.
Cit. Take him along.   He's sure game.

Her. You make no voolishness, you not arrest me.
Pol. Come on now, and the less talk the better. [*Exit.*

Enter CUNNINGHAM and JOHNSON, *carrying valises.*

Cun. He is to be tried before the colored Justice, Thomas Jefferson Wise. Wise has been in office but two weeks. O'Neil has gone to see him, and will try and have Herman discharged.

Enter PEABODY, *carrying valise.*

John. Peabody, did you hear of Ulrich's arrest.
Pea. No!
Cun. Yes, he has been arrested for selling goods without a city license, and is to be tried before Thomas Jefferson Wise, the colored Justice. O'Neil has gone to see his honor before the trial commences. We must take our valises to the hotel and go to hear the trial. The boys will all be there. Come on. [*Exit* JOHNSON, PEABODY and CUNNINGHAM.
Curtain.

SCENE V.—Office of Thomas Jefferson Wise, Justice of the Peace. —Furniture consists of a number of chairs and a large table covered with books.

Just. Wise. Mo' business, mo' law to be compounded by Judge Wise. Two weeks in office an' very 'portent cases hab arib and mo' still arib'en. No mo' old Jeff. now, but Judge Wise, de hono'ble court.

Enter O'NEIL.

O'Neil. [*Takes off hat and bows.*] Have I the pleasure of addressing the Honorable Thomas Jefferson Wise?
Just. Wise. Dis am de court whar de hono'ble Thomas Jefferson Wise prozides.
O'Neil. Judge Wise, I have come in the interest of one Herman Ulrich, who has been arrested for selling goods without a city license. Knowing you to be a wise interpreter and expounder of the constitution and laws of our country, I desire to make you a present [*Hands him a ten dollar bill.*] of some money, as a slight token of my appreciation of the decisions you have made, and the justice you have

awarded during the short time you have been in office. It is a custom now, and more particularly so here at the capital of the nation, to make presents to those holding high positions, the value of the presents always being less than the rewards returned by the very honorable gentlemen to whom the presents are made. I have not been able to find in the constitution of this great country where a state or a city has a right to impose a tax upon commerce, and visit your court for the purpose of hearing you decide that the law which brings Mr. Ulrich before you is unconstitutional, and to witness his discharge. Such a decision can but give you fame throughout the country, and insure you a rich reward from those most benefited by your wise interpretation of the law.

Just. Wise. De court will congest de law and decide in de spirit ob de cons'tution.

Enter POLICEMAN, HERMAN, CITIZENS, JOHNSON, PEABODY and others.

Just. Wise. De pris'ner heb'en arobe de congregation will obserb de stillness ob de 'casion, and de court will enter into de 'liberation ob de question now ariben for its congestion. De pris'ner before de table ob justice will now make confession ob guilt or not guilty.

Her. Ven I sbeak, I sbeak vot I sbeak ; ven I zay, I zay vot I zay ; ven I tole, I tole vot I dold you dot American eagle vas already one humbug. I zometimes dink dot American eagle vas no humbug, dot dat American eagle vas died or vas gone avay, an' do or dree buzzards vas gome und vos voolin' der beobles.   Dem ganderdate zay, goot Hons Michael dis land vos better den vos der Faderland ; dis vas der Liberdy land vere all der states vos vone, und der eagle schream ebluribus unum. I gome vrom New York vor zellin' goots vot der merchants vant, und ter bolice zay you are my brisoner. Vere vas dem eagle vot schream und schream ebluribus unum. Dem vos buzzards and geep sdill. In der Faderland it vos better den vas dot.   Neder vas it dot vay in Britishland vere dem lion roar. Dem ganderdate zay goot Hons Michael dis vas der Liberdy land, vere der beobles vos all vree, und der rich mans und der boor mans

vas ter zame pevore ter law, an' ven it pees not zo dem eagle schream an' schream und it must pe zo. Ven der var
gome an' der rich mans vat hafe dree hundred dollar sday
at home und der boor mans vot hafe no dree hundred dollar must go do der var; ven der law make der rich man's
dree hundred dollar zo goot as vos ter boor man's blood,
vere pees dem eagle vot schream an' schream zo loud.
Dem vos buzzards an' geep sdill. Dem ganderdate zay goot
Hons Michael dis vas better den vas der Faderland. In ter
Faderland it pees better den vas dot. Ven ter var gome in
ter Faderland money pies no mans vree. Ter brince an' ter
peasant pees der zame pevore der law an' vone alike as der
oder vollos der vlag of der Faderland do battle. Dem ganderdate zay goot Hons Michael in dis Liberdy land ter state
brodects der life of der citizen, und ven it pees not zo, dem
eagle schream an' schream und it must pe zo. Der mens
vot make der vines boisons dem vines do make more monies, der wholesale mens boisons dem vines do make more
monies, der redail mans boisons dem vines do make more
monies. Ven ter beobles vat pies dem vines vas boisoned
an' go mad; ven dem beobles vos died, vere pees dem eagle
vot schream an' schream zo loud. Dem vos buzzards und
geep sdill. In der Faderland it vos better den vas dat. In
der Faderland ter mans vot boison der vines an' gills der
beobles vas a griminal, und der vines vos bure. Ven dem
boloditions vot hold pig office zay sdealin' der beobles monies vas peesnis und liberdy vas der right vor do sdeal, vere
vas dem eagle vot schream an' schream zo loud. Dem vos
buzzards an' geep sdill. In der Faderland it vos bedder den
vos dot. In der Faderland der mans vot sdeal der beobles
monies vas a griminal. In der Faderland sdealin' der beobles monies vas not peesnis. Dem ganderdate zay goot
Hons Michael dem bolerditions vat hold pig office vas pad
but der beobles vos goot. It vas not dot vay. Ven der
rulers vos goot ter beobles vos goot; ven der rulers vos pad
den der beobles dink eif dem rulers do dat vay vey not we
do dot vay doo, und dem beobles got pad. Dem ganderdate zay goot Hons Michael dem eagle, dem eagle, dem eagle. I tole you vot I dold you dem vas buzzards; I tole you
vot I dold you dem eagle vas died or vas gone avay. [*Be-*

comes demonstrative and excited.] I tole you vot I dole you, vat I tole, vat I dole you— [O'NEIL *whispers to* HERMAN —HERMAN *stops suddenly and sits down.*

Just. Wise. De witness for de pers'cution ob de pris'ner will now be obserb'd by de court for his test'mony.

Cit. The prisoner was selling goods without a license.

Just. Wise. Did witness saw de pris'ner sellin' ob de goods?

Cit. No, but he couldn't show his license.

Just. Wise. De witness will take his seat and obserb de stillness ob de 'casion. De court will abstract test'mony from de next witness.

Pol. There is no more witnesses.

Just. Wise. De congregation will now obserb de stillness ob de 'casion. De ebidence ob de case hab'en been heard by de court, de court compounds de law and finds de pris'- ner not guilty ob de charge, and de law uncons'tutional 'cord- ing to de spirit ob de cons'tution ob dese United States, and de costs ob de trial to be liquidated by de witness for de pers'cution ob de pris'ner. De court hab now 'journed, and de stillness ob de 'casion hab ended. [*Applause. Curtain.*

SCENE VI.—Office of McMillan, Baxter & Armstead.—Armstead and Walters in the office.

Arm. [*Reading letter.*] Mr. Brown writes that he has been in Indianapolis ten days. He states that he will write us on Saturday and will reach home Monday or Tuesday, which will be to-day or to-morrow. [*Opens second letter.*] Have also a letter from Herman, enclosing several orders. Am sorry we cannot fill them. Herman will reach home to- day or to-morrow, and will bring his wife with him.

Wal. Herman married!

Arm. He says so.

Wal. If Baxter were here he would compliment him high- ly, and on his arrival would congratulate him very much.

Arm. No doubt. By the way, it is reported this morning that Baxter's father-in-law has failed. He was a heavy stock broker, and it may be that the late depression in stocks has been too much for him. The news, if true, will be hard for

Baxter to bear, not having an opportunity to over-draw as he did with us. He estimated his wife's wealth at three hundred thousand dollars, and I am sure does not believe in the longevity of fathers-in-law. If he had known that his father-in-law was about to fail he would have checked out all the money we had in bank. When he hears of the failure no doubt he will conclude to make his business trip of long duration. [*Opens third letter.*] We have notice that our depositions will be taken in the case of the State of Ohio *vs.* Washington Banks and Madison Weddel.

Enter McMILLAN.

McMil. I have spoken to R. B. Conger, and he will act as our Assignee. He knows the value of our goods and will be a suitable person. There ought to be at least one hundred thousand dollars left, after making allowance for shrinkage and paying all our indebtedness.

Arm. We have received letters from Mr. Brown and Herman. They will both reach home by to-morrow, and perhaps to-day. Herman is married and will bring his wife with him.

McMil. Herman married !

Arm. So he says,

McMil. He does not know of our failure, and I am afraid will not be able to find employment. He has done well during his trip, and with experience would make a good salesman. The merchants have confidence in him. I will do what I can for him. I have been informed that Baxter took with him five thousand dollars belonging to his church, in addition to the forty thousand stolen from us. It is reported this morning that Mr. Pool, Baxter's father-in-law, has failed.

Enter EXPRESS MESSENGER.

Mess. [*Opens package and counts money.*] McMillan, Baxter & Armstead: twenty-five thousand dollars, from Herman Ulrich. [WALTERS *pays express charges. Exit messenger.*

McMil. Can it be possible that Herman collected Banks & Weddel's note !

Arm. [*Reading letter.*] His letter states that the money was received from Banks & Weddel, in payment of their note.

Enter LETTER CARRIER.

Arm. [*Opens letter containing draft.*] More money. [*Reads letter.*

INDIANAPOLIS, JAN. 1877.
Messers. McMillan, Baxter & Armstead,
        Dear Sirs:—Enclosed find draft for fifty thousand dollars, in full of note against Wise & Morton.   It was all that I could do to secure the payment of the note.   They lost heavily in a grain speculation and could not avoid their failure.   They have the sympathy and respect of the people here.
                            Very respectfully yours,
                                            CHAS. BROWN.

McMil. Can it be possible! And Mr. Brown and Herman have saved me from bankruptcy.   Brown who has long been faithful to my interests and little rewarded, the man whom Aaron Baxter would have discharged.   Justice sooner or later, in this world or the world to come, is awarded unto all men, and justice will yet come unto Aaron Baxter.   Draw a check for one hundred and fifty thousand dollars, deposit the money we have received and lift our note.   I am going out but will return soon.   [*Exit* McMILLAN.

Enter Mr. and Mrs. BROWN and Mr. and Mrs. ULRICH.

Arm. [ARMSTEAD and WALTERS *welcome* Mr. and Mrs. BROWN, *welcome and congratulate* HERMAN, *and are introduced to his wife.*] Mr. McMillan stepped out but will return in a few minutes.

Enter McMILLAN.

McMil. [*Welcomes* Mr. and Mrs. BROWN, *welcomes and congratulates* HERMAN, *and is introduced to his wife.*] We welcome you all home.   We have had troubles of late, but the sky is brightening again.   Mr. Baxter has left us, and by so doing has given room for those more deserving.   To-morrow it will be made known that Aaron Baxter is no longer with us, and that the late firm of McMillan, Baxter & Armstead will hereafter be known under the firm name of McMillan, Armstead & Co., the members of the new firm will be George W. McMillan, Robert B. Armstead, Charles

Brown and Charles F. H. Ulrich.   I am getting old, and the business of the new firm will devolve principally upon my partners.   I will furnish the capital to conduct the business, and will charge six per cent interest for the use of the money.   The profits will be equally divided among the four partners.   When capital is rewarded by labor, labor in return should be rewarded by capital.   [*Curtain.*

THE END.

www.ingramcontent.com/pod-product-compliance
Lightning Source LLC
Chambersburg PA
CBHW031803090426
42739CB00008B/1145